D1545644

THE DIVINE ROMANCE

The Divine Romance

FULTON J. SHEEN

ALBA·HOUSE   NEW·YORK

SOCIETY OF ST. PAUL, 2187 VICTORY BLVD., STATEN ISLAND, NEW YORK 10314

Library of Congress Cataloging-in-Publication Data

Sheen, Fulton J. (Fulton John), 1895-1979.
    The divine romance / Fulton J. Sheen. — Alba House ed.
        p.   cm.
    Originally published: New York: Century Co., 1930.
    ISBN 0-8189-0781-9
    1. Catholic Church — Apologetic works.   I. Title.
    BX1752.S52   1996
    230'.2 — dc20   96-32566
                                                                    CIP

Nihil Obstat:
Arthur Scanlon, STD
Censor Librorum

Imprimatur:
Partrick Cardinal Hayes
✠ Archbishop of New York
October 24, 1930

The Nihil Obstat and Imprimatur are official declarations
that a book or pamphlet is free of doctrinal or moral
error. No implication is contained therein that those
who have granted the Nihil Obstat and Imprimatur agree
with the contents, opinions or statements expressed.

This Alba House edition is published by special arrangement
with the Estate of Fulton J. Sheen and the Society for the
Propagation of the Faith, 366 Fifth Avenue, New York, NY 10001.

This book is published in the United States of America
by Alba House, the publishing arm of the Society of St. Paul,
an international religious congregation of priests and brothers
serving the Church through the communications media.

ISBN: 0-8189-0781-9

Printing Information:

Current Printing - first digit   1   2   3   4   5   6   7   8   9   10

Year of Current Printing - first year shown

1996   1997   1998   1999   2000   2001   2002   2003

In Thanks To
Mary Immaculate
Mother of God
Seat of Wisdom

Table of Contents

Author's Introduction

The material in this book, *The Divine Romance*, forms a unity, beginning as it does with the quest for Life and Truth and Love which is to be found in God. In the second chapter some attempt is made, with the aid of revelation, to learn something of the inner Life of God. In the third chapter, Love is revealed as going outside of itself and creating a moral universe, and in the fourth, Love appears personally to restore the pristine beauty of the moral universe. The last three chapters show how Love Incarnate, which is Christ Himself, continues to *live* in His new Body, which is the Church; to *die* through sin on the part of those who "crucify Christ again in their souls," and finally to *rise again* in the permanency of His Church with which He abides even to the consummation of the world.

The book is in no sense controversial, seeking as it does to be to a mind what bread is to a starving man. It has already been preached from the "house-tops"; it now remains to be written on the fleshy tablets of human hearts, and if one single heart permits that message to be written on it by the finger of God, the author will feel that much will already have been done to make this world a better place in which to live.

In the preparation of this book the author used a few ideas which were incorporated in his preceding work, *The Life of All Living*. Special thanks are due to the National Council of Catholic Men, which printed this material as a pamphlet, and which has graciously permitted its publication in book form.

MAN'S QUEST FOR GOD

Man's Quest for God

The quest for God is essentially the search for the full account and meaning of life. If we but had the power to take our soul from our body, put it in a crucible, and distil out the meaning of that quest, what would we find it to be? If we could but make the inmost heart of all humanity speak out its inmost yearnings, what would we discover them to be? Would we not find that every heart and mind and soul in creation desires fundamentally three realities and only three — Life, Truth, and Love? In fact, so deep are these three realities, Being, Truth and Love, that we can say the whole universe overflows with them. Of each thing in the universe it can be said that it *is*. Of each thing in the universe it can be said that it is *true*, for it is related to a mind. Of each thing in the universe it can be said that it is *love*, for it is related to a will and a desire.

The first deep-seated yearning, then, in the human heart is the yearning for *Life*. Of all our treasures it is that which we surrender last, and with the greatest reluctance. Titles, joys, and wealth, power, ambition, honor — all of these we will let go provided we can hold on to that precious, palpitating, vibrating thing called life. The very instinct which impels us to put out our hand when we walk in the dark, proves that we are willing to sacrifice a part of our body rather than to endanger that which we hold most precious — our life. Not even the sad fact of suicide disproves the reality of this yearning, for in every suicide there is an illusion and a sentiment. The illusion is that suicide is total destruction. The sentiment is the desire for repose or the will to shake off the worries of life. Suicide is not so much the desire that one wants to be annihilated, but rather that one wants to be at ease, which is just another way of saying one wants to have a different life.

The second most fundamental craving is the desire for *Truth*. The very first question we asked when we came into this world was the question "Why?"; a question which betrays that we are all born incipient philosophers. As children, we tear apart our toys to find out what makes the wheels go round. As grown-ups, never having lost the desire to know the "Why" and "Wherefore" of things, we tear apart, by our mental analysis, the very toy of the universe to find out what makes its wheels go round. We turn our telescopes on the sun and ask it to divulge its secrets; we ask the stars to tell us the story of their twinkling; and the very ocean to surrender the mystery of its depth. We are incurably bent on knowing and discovering the truth of things — that is why we hate to have secrets kept from us.

But that is not all. The third fundamental inclination of human nature is the desire to *Love* and to be loved. From the first day in the Garden of Eden, when God said: "It is not good for man to be alone," on even to the crack of doom, man has thirsted and will thirst for love. Each child that is born into the world instinctively presses itself to its mother's breast in testimony of affection. Later on he goes to his mother to have his play-wounds bound, and to shed his tears down the cheek of his mother. Finally, when the child has grown to man's estate, he looks for a companion, young like himself, one to whom he can "unpack his heart with words"; one who will measure up to that beautiful definition of friendship, "one in whose presence we can keep silence" — it is only before strangers that we must speak. Then the love of spouse for spouse is sealed in the bonds of matrimony, and when monotony threatens its sanctity, then there comes a child which makes an earthly Trinity. Thus the love of parents for children becomes the love of grandparents for grandchildren, and so the quest goes on from the cradle to the grave.

We desire life and truth and love, but do we find them in their plenitude on this earth? Do we carry within ourselves the energy, the force, and the power to realize them to the highest degree? Are we such masters and captains of our fate that we may give to ourselves an overflowing measure of these most precious of all gifts? We possess a fraction of life, a fraction of truth, and a fraction of love, but do we possess them in their fullness?

Certainly life is not completely under our control. Successes of life are soon exhausted. Reputations wane and are forgotten. Schemes have their hour and come to naught. The science of one age is superseded by that of another. The taste of one age is unintelligible to the next. Poets become silent. Each tick of the clock brings us closer to the tomb; "our hearts are but muffled drums beating a funeral march to the grave." "From hour to hour we ripe and ripe; from hour to hour we rot and rot." Life may be a great torrent outpoured from the inexhaustible chalice of eternity, but we are permitted but a few drops of it in the cup of our own life.

And although truth is a condition of our nature, neither do we possess it in its fullness, for the more we study the less we know, or rather the less we think we know. Learning opens up a thousand new vistas of knowledge down which we might travel for a lifetime, if we had a thousand lives. What man is there who has devoted his life to study who will not honestly avow that he really knows less now than what he thought he knew the night he graduated from high school? How often, too, the search for truth corrects the prejudices of youth, and how often earnest seekers after truth have come to mock and remain to pray? Great minds like Newton have confessed that all their knowledge seemed to leave them standing on the seashore of truth before which stretched an ocean of infinite truth. Thomas Aquinas, the greatest mind the world has ever produced, declared at the end of his life that all that he wrote seemed to him as straw compared to a vision which Divine Truth had accorded him.

Finally, love in its perfect state is not to be found in this world. Broken hearts, ruined homes, young widows, divorce courts, orphans —all are so many eloquent proofs that man has not found a true and lasting love. Unfortunately, with the passing of time it often loses its delicacy. How rare, for example, is the young man who can treasure for days and for weeks and for years the gift of a rose or the touch of a hand of a friend. Quaff as he will the magic of love's wine and drink deep as he may of her springs, a day must finally come when the last cake is crumbled at life's great feast, and the last embrace is passed from friend to friend. The noblest and best of human love ends, and nothing is perfect that ends.

Though we are the lord and master of the universe, though we possess these strong yearnings, which are the very mainsprings of our beings, yet we do not find these yearnings fulfilled on this earth. Life is mingled with death; truth is mingled with error; and love is mingled with hate. Our life, then, is not in creatures; our truth, then, is not in the spoken word; our love, then, is not in what we see. Life cannot exist with death; truth cannot exist with error; and love cannot exist with hate.

But where find the source of these three realities? Where find the author of existence and truth and love that vibrates through all creation? Shall we say that they have no source? But, if they have no source, how can they be, and how can they affect our lives at this moment? They are things that are reasonable and, therefore, must have been intelligently produced. They cannot come from the dismal slime of primeval jungles, for then the mind would be confronted with the absurdity that the nobler comes from the less noble. Where, then, find their source?

Suppose I am in search of the source of the light which is in this room. Where shall I find it? The source of the light is not to be found under that distant chair, for there light is mingled with shadow. The source of the light is not to be found under the table, for there too light is mingled with darkness. Where find the source of light? I must go out to something which is nothing but pure light, namely, the sun. So, too, if I am to find the source of the life and the truth and the love that is in this world, I must go out to a Life that is not mingled with the shadow, death; I must go out to a Truth which is not mingled with the shadow, error; and I must go out to a Love which is not mingled with the shadow, hate. I must go out beyond "the margent of this world," out past the "golden gateways of the stars," out past the clotted clay of all humanity, out even to the "hid battlements of eternity," out to Some One who is Pure Life, Pure Truth, and Pure Love.

> "There is a quest that calls me
> In nights when I am alone,
> The need to ride where the ways divide
> The Known from the Unknown.

> "I mount what thought is near me
> And soon I reach the place,
> The tenuous rim where the Seen grows dim,
> And the sightless hides its face.

> "I have ridden the wind,
> I have ridden the sea,
> I have ridden the moon and stars,
> I have set my feet in the stirrup seat
> Of a comet coursing Mars.

> "And everywhere
> Thro' the earth and air
> My thought speeds, lightning-shod,
> It comes to a place where checking pace
> It cries 'Beyond lies God.'"

Oh, would that I had the speech of angel tongues or the language which Adam spoke in Eden, or a tongue like Isaiah which had been touched with a coal from the very altar of God — then, perhaps, I could make you understand what God is. But our untempered speech which descends "grimy and rough-cast from Babel's bricklayers," strong it is to damn, strong it is to speak of cheek and lip and bosom; for these things it moves with light ease in the speech of the working day. But to speak of God: it moves with the clumsiness of the hieroglyphs. Poor as it is, language may tell its story that God is not some dim far-off abstraction, not some "spatio-temporal configuration"; not "an epochal occasion"; not an energy, but the fullness of Life and Truth and Love.

God is that Life which has throbbed throughout the agelessness of eternity, wherein each moment is eternity and eternity is as a moment; that Life whence has come all existing things from the stars, the "glimmering tapers lit about the day's dead sanctities," on even to the smiling face of a babe in a crib.

God is that Truth in Whom darkness and ignorance can find no place, before Whom all is spread out in its widest extent and smallest detail; that Truth the Greek academicians sought as they walked the streets of Athens, the Truth the scientist seeks as he uncovers fossils in the strata of the earth, the Truth the saint seeks as he leaves the lights and glamors of the world for the shades and shadows of the cross where saints are made.

God is that Love Who ever wills and loves the Good because it is His nature, that Love whence has come the love of spouse for spouse, and that yet stranger love of a Stephen who loved and prayed for those who stoned him in hate; and the purer love of "passionless passion and mild tranquilities" wherein the heart confides in God alone.

If, then, God is the source of the Life, the Truth, and the Love in the universe, and if the very existence of these things depends more upon Him than the evening rays upon the setting sun, do we not owe Him something in return? If there are gifts, shall there not be gratitude for gifts? If a man invents a machine, does not the government give him patent rights entitling him to returns on his invention? If an author writes a book, is he not entitled to royalties on his writings, simply because they are the creation of his mind? Now, we are God's invention, or better still, God's creation. Is not God, therefore, entitled to a return on His creation? Is He not entitled to royalties on His works? And since He has given us three great gifts which contain all other gifts, should He not be entitled to triple returns on those gifts? Since He gave us Truth, are we not in duty bound to know Him? Since He gave us Love, should we not love in return? Since He gave us Life, should we not serve Him? If we admit that triple bond, then we admit religion, or commerce between God and man, and such is the first lesson of the penny catechism:

"Why did God make us?" "God made us to know Him, to love Him, to serve Him in this world and to be happy with Him forever in heaven."

Thus I come back to my starting point: The quest for God is essentially the search for the full account and meaning of life. And life has a meaning because the essence of God is Love.

God is not a Being who does not know how to love; not one of those tepid hearts that have no flames, and whose tiny sparks have not the power of enkindling others, but fly back only upon themselves; not a powerless God who knows how to love but cannot realize His dreams; not a God who burns with love but has only cold words to say. God's love is not like a stream which runs deep and mighty as long as it is held within narrow banks, but like the great Feast at which five thousand sat and all did have their fill.

If we would know what God is, then we need only look into our own hearts. Something Godlike is mirrored there — for whatever is best in the treasured lives of heroic men and the serene unwritten lives of innocent women; whatever is best in the loyalty of human hearts and the unwearying sweetness of a mother's love; whatever is noble in the sacrificing care of a father and the devotion of an unselfish friend, is but the dim reflection, the far-off echo, the faint shadow of that which in God is perfect. We are but enjoying a two-billionth part of the light and heat which streams from the sun, and it may equally be that we are receiving even a smaller fraction of the Love and Life and Truth which is in God.

Do not think that any heart can speak with such a rapturous language but that there is a deeper heart, a greater love, and a nobler affection. If your own mother seems to you to be the incarnation of all that is loving in life, do you think the God who made mothers can be any less loving? If your own father seems to you to be the realization of all that kindness in life can mean, do you think the God who made fathers is any less kind? If your own heart and mind revel in the size of the planets and the nature of the spheres, do you not think it should thrill at the knowledge of Him before whom all the nations of the earth are poised as the grains in the balance? If there are times when the joy of living almost transports us into other realms; if there are times when the discovery of a human truth lifts us into heights of ecstatic repose; if there are times when the human heart in its noblest reaches and purest affections has the power to cast us into an ecstasy, to thrill and exalt us, then what must be the great Heart of hearts! If a human heart can increase the joy of living, then what must be the great Heart of God! *If the Spark is so bright, oh, what must be the Flame!*

THE BLESSED TRINITY

The Blessed Trinity

The burden of the last message was that man is engaged in a threefold quest, for life, truth and love, and since he cannot find these in their fullness on this earth, because here life is mingled with death, truth with error, and love with hate, he must go out beyond the "margent of this world," out to Some One who is pure Life, pure Truth, and pure Love, which is God.

But this knowledge of God which came from reason working in the visible things of the world gives a very incomplete concept of Him. It is like the knowledge any one might gain of an artist by look-ing at his painting. But I could look at that painting from now until the crack of doom and I would never know anything of the artist's inmost thoughts and loves, hopes and aspirations. I could know these only by a personal revelation on his part.

In like manner I can know something of the existence of God, something of His Infinite Power, Life, and Beauty by contemplating His universe, but I could never divine anything of His secret Thought and Love. His creation gives but dim hints of these.

It was therefore only natural that man should desire further knowledge of the inner life of God, and in seeking that light would ask such questions as Plato asked four centuries before Christ:

"If there is only one God, what does He think about, for if He is an intelligent being He must think of something?

"If there is only one God, whom does He love? And to be happy one must love."

These questions were hurled against the high heavens as so much brass, for there was no man to give them an answer. The answer could come only from God Himself and it came when Our Blessed Lord appeared on earth and revealed to us the inmost life of God, when He told us there were three Persons in God, God the Father, God the Son, and God the Holy Spirit. This tremendous mystery, known as the mystery of the Trinity — the mystery which answers the questions of Plato, which is above reason and yet not contrary to it — with the help of revelation and analogy, I shall try to explain to you.

If we would answer the questions of Plato and know what God thinks about, and whom God loves, let us first ask the questions of man, for man has been made to the image and likeness of God. The study of man's thought and man's will will tell us something about the thought and the will of God.

Of the thought of man three things may be

said, viz.: It is a word; it is generated or born; and finally it is personal.

Man thinks; he thinks a thought such as "Justice," "Faith," "Fortitude," or "Charity." Now these thoughts are words; they are words even before I speak them, for the vocal word is only the expression of the internal word in my mind.

These thoughts or internal words are generated or born. Who, for example, ever sat down to a meal with "Justice"? Who ever heard of "Charity" going out for a walk? Who knows the size, the weight, and the color of "Fortitude"? No one has ever seen, tasted, or touched these thoughts, and yet they are real. They are spiritual thoughts, therefore. But where did they come from? Since they are not wholly in the outside world, they must have been produced, or generated by the mind itself, not with that physical birth by which animal produces animal, but that spiritual generation by which we produce ideas or internal words. There are other ways of begetting life, we must remember, than the mere physical ways we see in the world about us. The most chaste way that life is begotten is the way in which thoughts and ideas are born in the mind.

Finally, the thought of man may be personal. Some thoughts of man are banal and commonplace, trite thoughts which no man remembers; but there are also thoughts which are spirit and life. There are some thoughts of man into which man puts his very soul and his very being, all that he has been and all that he is, which thoughts are so much the thoughts of that thinker, as to carry his personality and his spirit with them, so that we can recognize them as thoughts of that person; thus, we say, that is a thought of Pascal, of Bossuet, of Shakespeare, or of Dante.

Now apply these three reflections about human thought to God. God thinks a thought, and that thought is a Word; it is generated or born and is therefore called a Son, and finally, that Word or Son is Personal.

God thinks: He thinks a Thought. This thought of God is a Word, as my own thought is called a word after it is pronounced. It is an internal word. But God's thought is not like ours. It is not multiple. God does not think one Thought, or one Word, one minute and another the next. Thoughts are not born to die, and do not die to be reborn in the mind of God. All is present to Him at once. In Him there is only one Word. He has no need of another. That thought or Word is infinite and equal to Himself, unique and absolute, first-born of the Spirit of God; a Word which tells what God is, a Word from which all human words have been derived, and of which created things are but merely the broken syllables or letters; a Word which is the source of all the Wisdom in the world. The latest scientific discoveries, the new knowledge of the great expanse of the heavens, the sciences of biology, physics, and chemistry, the more lofty ones of metaphysics, philosophy, and theology, the knowledge of the Shepherds, and the knowledge of the Wise Men — all this knowledge has its Source in the Word or the Wisdom of God.

The Infinite Thought of God is called not only a Word to indicate that it is the Wisdom of God, but is also called a Son because it has been generated or begotten. The Thought or the Word of God does not come from the outside world; it is born in His Spirit in a much more perfect way than the thought of "Justice" is generated by my own spirit. The giving of life or the power of birth, I repeat, is not limited to human beings. In the language of Sacred Scripture, "Shall not I Who make others bring forth children Myself bring forth, said the Lord? Shall I Who give generation to others Myself be barren?" The ultimate Source of all generation or birth is God, whose Word is born of Him and therefore is called a Son. Just as in our own human order, the principle of all generation is called the Father, so too, in the Trinity the principle of spiritual generation is called the Father, and the one born is called the Son, because He is the perfect Image and Resemblance of the Father. If an earthly father can transmit to his son all the nobility of his character, and all the fine traits of his life, how much more so can the Heavenly Father communicate to His own Eternal Son all the nobility, the perfection, and the Eternity of His Being!

Finally, this Word or Son, born of the Eternal God, is personal. The Thought of God is not commonplace, but reaches to the abyss of all that is known or can be known. Into this Thought or Word God puts Himself so entirely that this Thought or Word is as living as Himself, perfect as Himself, infinite as Himself. If a human genius can put his whole personality into a thought, in a more perfect way God is able to put so much of Himself into a thought that that Thought or Word or Son is conscious of Himself and is a Divine Person.

The Father does not first exist and then think; the Father and Son are coeternal, for in God all is present and unchanging. Nothing is new and nothing is lost. Thus it is that the Father, contemplating His Image, His Word, His Son, can say in the ecstasy of the first and real paternity, "You are My Son; this day I have begotten You." "This day" —this day of eternity, that is, the indivisible duration of being without end. "This day," in that act that will never end as it has never begun; this day — the agelessness of eternity.

Go back to the origin of the world, pile century on century, aeon on aeon, age on age: "The Word was with God." Go back before the creation of the angels, before Michael summoned his war hosts to victory and there was a flash of archangelic spears; even then, "The Word was with God." It is that Word which St. John heard in the beginning of his Gospel, when he wrote: "In the beginning was the Word: and the Word was with God; and the Word was God," and just as my interior thoughts are not made manifest without a word, so the Word in the language of John, "became flesh and dwelt among us." And that Word is no other than the Second Person of the Blessed Trinity, the Word who embraces the beginning and end of all things; the Word who existed before creation; the Word who presided at creation as the King of the Universe, the Word made flesh at Bethlehem, the Word made flesh on the cross, and the Word made flesh dwelling with divinity and humanity in the Eucharistic Emmanuel. The Good Friday of twenty centuries ago did not mark the end of Him, as it did not mark the beginning. It is one of the moments of the Eternal Word of God. Jesus Christ has a prehistory — the only prehistory that is prehistory, a prehistory not to be studied in the rocks of the earth, not in the caves of man, not in the slime and dust of primeval jungles, but in the bosom of an eternal Father; He alone brought history to history; He alone has dated all the records of human events ever since into two periods: the period before and the period after His coming; so that if we would ever deny that the Word became flesh, and that the Son of God became the Son of man, we would have to date our denial as over one thousand nine hundred years after His coming.

We are not yet finished with the inner life of

God, for if God is the source of all life and truth and goodness in the world, He must have a will as well as an intellect; a love as well as a thought. It is a fact of nature that every being loves its own perfection. The perfection of the eye is color, and it loves the beauty of the sun setting in the flaming monstrance of the west; the perfection of the ear is sound, and it loves the harmony of an overture of Beethoven or a sonata of Chopin. Love has two terms: He who loves and He who is loved. In love the two are reciprocal. I love and I am loved. Between me and the one I love there is a bond. It is not my love; it is not his love; it is our love; the mysterious resultant of two affections, a bond which enchains, and an embrace wherein two hearts leap with but a single joy. The Father loves the Son, the Image of His Perfection and the Son loves the Father. Love is not only in the Father. Love is not only in the Son. There is something between them, as it were. The Father loves the Son, whom He engenders. The Son loves the Father, who engendered Him. They contemplate each other; love each other; unite in a love so powerful, so strong, and so perfect that it forms between them a living bond. They give themselves in a love so infinite that, like the truth which expresses itself only in the giving of a whole personality, their love can express itself in nothing less than a Person, who is Love. Love at such a stage does not speak; does not cry; does not express itself by words, nor by canticles; it expresses itself as we do in some ineffable moments, by that which indicates the very exhaustion of our giving: namely, a sigh, or a breath — and that is why the Third Person of the Blessed Trinity is called the Holy Spirit.

That breath of love is not a passing one as our own, but an Eternal Spirit. How all this is done, I do not know, but on the testimony of God revealing, I know that this same Holy Spirit overshadowed the Blessed Virgin Mary, and He who was born of her was called the Son of God; it was the same Spirit of whom our Lord spoke to Nicodemus when He told him he must be born again of "water and the Holy Spirit"; it was the same Spirit whom our Blessed Savior gave to His apostles with the words, "Receive the Holy Spirit: whose sins you shall forgive, they are forgiven them"; it was the same Spirit of whom our Lord spoke at the Last Supper: "He will glorify Me, because He will take from what is mine and declare it to you. Everything that the Father has is mine." In this passage Christ tells His disciples that the Holy Spirit, who is to come, will in the future reveal divine knowledge which has been communicated to Him in His procession from both the Father and Son. It is that same Spirit who, in fulfillment of the promise "but when the Spirit of Truth comes, He will teach you all truth," descended on the Apostles on the day of Pentecost, and became the soul of the Church. And I believe that the continuous, unbroken succession of the truth communicated by Christ to His Church has survived to our own day, not because of the human organization of the Church, for that is carried on by frail vessels, but because of the profusion of the Spirit of Love and Truth over Christ's Vicar, and all who belong to Christ's mystical Body, which is His Church.

Three in one, Father, Son, and Holy Spirit; three Persons in one God; one in essence, distinction of persons, such is the mystery of the Trinity, such is the inner life of God. Just as I am, I know, and I love, and yet I am one; as the three angles of a triangle do not make three triangles but one; as the heat, power, and light of the sun do not make three suns, but one; as water, ice, and steam are all manifestations of the one substance; as the form, color, and perfume of the rose do not make three roses, but one; as our soul, our intellect, and our will do not make three substances, but one; as one times one times one does not equal three, but one, so too in some much more mysterious way, there are three Persons in God and yet only one God.

The Trinity is the answer to the questions of Plato. If there is only one God, what does He think about? He thinks an eternal thought, or about His Eternal Son. If there is only one God, whom does He love? He loves His Son, and that mutual love is the Holy Spirit. I firmly believe that the great philosopher was fumbling about for the mystery of the

Trinity, for his great mind seemed in some small way to suspect that an infinite being must have relations of thought and love, and that God cannot be conceived without thought and love. But it was not until the Word became Incarnate that man knew the secret of those relations and the inner life of God.

It is that mystery of the Trinity which gives the answer to those who have pictured God as an egotist God, sitting in solitary splendor before the world began, reduced to love Himself as a selfish deity. The Trinity is a revelation that before creation, God enjoyed the amiable society of His three Persons, the infinite communion with Truth and the embrace of infinite Love, and hence had no need ever to go outside of Himself in search for happiness. The greatest wonder of all is that, being perfect and enjoying perfect happiness, He ever should have made a world. And if He did make a world, He could only have had one motive for making it. It could not add to His perfection; it could not add to His Truth; it could not increase His happiness. He made a world only because He loved.

Finally, it is the mystery of the Trinity which gives the answer to the quest for our happiness and the meaning of heaven. Heaven is not a place where there is the mere vocal repetition of alleluias or the monotonous fingering of harps. Heaven is a place where we find the fullness of all the fine things we enjoy on this earth. Heaven is a place where we find in its plenitude those things which slake the thirst of hearts, satisfy the hunger of starving minds, and give rest to unrequited love. Heaven is the communion with perfect Life, perfect Truth, and perfect Love, God the Father, God the Son, and God the Holy Spirit to whom be all honor and glory for ever and ever. Amen.

LOVE'S OVERFLOW

Love's Overflow

Away back in the agelessness of eternity, in that day that had neither beginning nor end, God was enjoying infinite communion with Truth and Love in the amiable society of the three Persons of the Trinity: Father, Son, and Holy Spirit. Wanting nothing for His perfection, desiring nothing for His happiness, needing nothing for the replenishing of His life, there was no need for God ever to go outside of Himself. If, therefore, He ever chose to create a world, it must have been not on account of need, nor duty, nor constraint, but only on account of love.

Why then did God create a world? God created the world for something like the same reason that we find it hard to keep a secret! Good things are hard to keep. The rose is good, and tells its secret in perfume. The sun is good, and tells its secret in light and heat. Man is good, and tells the secret of his goodness in the language of thought. But God is infinitely good and therefore infinitely loving. Why therefore could not He by a free impulsion of His love let love overflow and bring new worlds into being? God could not keep, as it were, the secret of His love, and the telling of it was creation.

Love overflowed. Eternity moved and said to time, "Begin." Omnipotence moved and said to nothingness, "Be." Light moved and said to darkness, "Be light." Out from the fingertips of God there tumbled planets and worlds. Stars were thrown into their orbits and the spheres into space. Orbs and brotherhoods of orbs began to fill the heavens. The great march of the world began, in which planet passes by planet and sphere by sphere, without ever a hitch or a halt. In that long procession of the unfolding of the creative power of God, there came first matter, then palpitating life and the paradise of Creation with its fourfold rivers flowing through all lands rich with gold and onyx, and finally those creatures made not by a Fiat but by a council of the Trinity — the first man and woman.

Quite naturally the mind of that great architect might have conceived ten thousand other possible worlds than this. This is not absolutely the best world that God could have made. But it is the best world for the purpose that He had in mind in making it. Almighty God chose to make a universe in which not all the creatures would be like sticks and stones, trees and beasts, each of which is impelled by a law of nature, or a law of instinct to a determined rigorous end, without the slightest enjoyment of freedom. He willed to place in paradise a creature made to His own image and likeness, but a creature different from all others, because endowed with that glorious gift of freedom, which is the power of saying "Yes" or "No," of choosing to sacrifice oneself to duty or duty to oneself, and forever remaining master and captain of one's own fate and destiny. In other words, God willed to make a moral universe, and the only condition upon which morality is possible is freedom.

In the very nature of things, ethics and morality can exist only upon the condition of a veto. Bravery, for example, is possible only in a world in which a man may be a coward. Virtue is possible only in a world where a man may be vicious. Sacrifice is possible only in that order in which a man may be selfish. Love is possible only when it is possible not to love. Cold statues cannot love. It is the possibility of saying "No" which gives so much charm to the heart when it says "Yes." A victory may be celebrated only on those fields in which a battle may be lost. Hence, in the divine order of things, God made a world in which man and woman would rise to moral heights, not by that blind driving power which makes the sun rise each morning, but rather by the exercise of that freedom in which one may fight the good fight and enjoy the spoils of victory, for no one shall be crowned unless he has struggled.

God in His goodness did not choose simply to

make a man moral and then give him merely the moral rewards to which a man is naturally entitled. He willed to do more than this. When a man becomes a father, is he content merely to give his child only that which is necessary? Does he not rather as a loving father give to his son even more than that which is his due? So, in like manner God willed to give man certain gifts of body and soul which far exceeded the nature or the capacity of man. Imagine a wealthy banker who would form a trust fund for a foundling baby, in which a vast sum of money was to be paid to the child when he reached the age of twenty-one, provided that during that time he led a good moral life. Now God established some such trust fund. He willed to give to the first man and woman certain gifts which would be theirs permanently, and for their posterity, providing that they proved faithful in their love. Among these gifts were *immunity from disease and death*, *freedom from the rebellion of flesh over reason*, and above all a gift of *knowledge* which far surpassed reason and enabled man to grasp divine truths in a far greater way than a telescope reveals to the eye the distant stars and planets; and a gift of *power or grace* which made the first man and woman not mere creatures of the handiwork of God, but God's own children, and co-heirs with Him in the kingdom of heaven. These gifts, be it understood, were even less due to the nature of man than the power of blooming

belongs to marble, or the song of a poet belongs to
a beast.

But these gifts were conditioned, for the universe is moral. They could be kept on one condition,
namely, by loving God. And loving God means
loving what is best for ourselves. But how try love?
The only way to try love is in a trial which forces one
to declare it. The only way for Adam and Eve as free
moral beings to prove their love and gratitude to
God was by choosing Him in preference to all else,
and admitting that their added knowledge and their
added power or grace were gifts. A double condition
was laid upon them to test their love. The first part
of the condition was *obscure*; it gave them an oppor-
tunity to admit that the added knowledge was a gift
of God. The second part was *reserved*; it allowed
them to admit that the added power of the will was
a gift of God. Thus they would show that they loved
God with their whole mind and their whole will, and
preferred Him to all things else. In concrete terms,
the trial was that they might enjoy all the riches of
the garden of paradise, but the fruit of one tree — the
tree of the knowledge of good and evil — they were
not to touch. God did not say *why* they should not
— and that was the *obscure* point on which their
intelligence was tried. Man should believe God on
this point as on all others. God *did* say they must
abstain from the fruits of that tree. That was the
reserved point which was the trial of their will. God

was imposing a limit to the sovereignty of man, reminding him that if he did the one thing forbidden he would imperil all the things provided, and that, like Pandora later on, if he should open the forbidden box, he would lose his treasures and let loose confusion worse confounded on the world.

The story of the fall as recorded in Genesis is known to all. Satan, appearing in the form of a serpent, tempted Eve with the question that destroyed confidence, which is the root of all love. "Did God really tell you not to eat from any of the trees in the garden? [Don't you know that] the moment you eat of [the tree in the middle of the garden] your eyes will be opened and you will be like gods who know what is good and what is bad?" Eve looks at the forbidden fruit; it is beautiful to behold. More and more she turns herself from the voice and thought of God to the fragrancy and imagined sweetness of the forbidden fruit. The lingering thought passes into a vivid imagination, the vivid imagination into a burning wish, the burning wish into a half-formed purpose, the half-formed purpose into a hasty act. Swiftly the crisis is upon her, as all such crises are, and the deed was done irrevocably until time shall be no more. She gave the forbidden fruit to Adam, and pride and self-will entered into his heart. He wanted to show he too knew what was good for him, and that his mind need not be kept obscured on any one point, nor his will reserved by any one condition. He wanted to be independent and show that he could do what he liked. And so he ate the fruit which he was forbidden to eat, because it was fair, and still more to show his own independence. Surely, this is understandable. Have we not done the same thing in our own lives over and over again? When we were children, were we not forbidden to do something which we wished to do? Did we not long for it and determine to have it all the more because it was forbidden? Adam did it for the very same reason, and that act of disobedience by which Adam failed the test of love is the first sin of this created universe, the sin which infected humanity in its origin and the sin which, for that reason, has been called original sin.

The whole trial was perfectly reasonable. Imagine a wealthy man who owns a beautiful estate. He tells his chauffeur and the chauffeur's wife that he will permit them to live in his mansion, ride in his motorcars, use his servants, enjoy his yacht, play about his spacious gardens, eat at his expense. In a word, they are to enjoy everything — provided that they will not touch a certain oil painting that hangs in one of his drawing rooms. Now, if the lady persuaded the gentleman to touch that painting, she would not be a lady, and if the gentleman touched the painting at the suggestion of the lady, he would not be a gentleman. By doing the one thing forbidden, they would lose all the things provided, and who would accuse the master of the house of injustice if he no longer permitted them to enjoy his gifts?

The doctrine, then, of the fall of man is far from the travesty made upon it by frivolous minds who would have the ordinance of God repose solely on an apple, for to do this is to miss the point of the whole story. To speak of the fall does not mean merely a garden and a serpent; to say that it is much more than any garden or any snake is not the same as saying there was no garden and there was no snake. It is simply saying what is of primary and what is of secondary importance; what is primary is the respect due to God, the fruit of the tree being the symbol of that respect. To make light of the fruit of a tree under such circumstances is just as rash as to make light of the flag of our country, as a symbol of our country's sovereignty. A flag stands for a nation, and the hand that carries it would retain it at the cost of a thousand deaths rather than let it be seized and desecrated by the enemy. It may be a small thing to violate a cloth that is red and white and blue, but it is no small thing to desecrate that for which it stands. So, likewise, in the terrestrial paradise, the famous tree in which God summarized all the knowledge of good and evil was a symbol, a moral limit which God imposed on the sovereignty of man to prove his obedience and his love. To say it was only a fable is to miss the great truth that things — a handshake or a smile, for example — may not only be, but may also signify.

There are three points that I would make in conclusion concerning the fall of man. The first is that by this act of disobedience, which is called his original sin, man lost nothing which was due to him or to his nature. He lost only gifts, and became, as St. Augustine has said, "just mere man." On Christmas Day when you distribute gifts to your friends, a person with whom you are unacquainted would not dare come to you and argue that you had refused to give him gifts as you had given them to your friends. Your answer would be: "Sir, I have done you no injustice. I have deprived you of nothing which is your due. I have even given to my friends that which was not theirs." And so it is with original sin. In losing the gifts of God, man lost nothing which was due to his nature. He was reduced to a state in which God might possibly have created him, with the difference that the loss of the gifts weakened his intellect and will, but did not make his nature intrinsically corrupt. Imagine a line of soldiers; notice one of these in particular. He resembles all the others in dress, appearance, and action, but yesterday he was an officer, thanks to a political preferment rather than to meritorious advancement. For an act of misdemeanor he was degraded and the badge of his office was taken from him. He was reduced to the state in which you see him now. Original sin, then, is not to be in the state we are in, but to have fallen into that state.

Secondly, this sin of Adam was not merely the sin of an individual, it was the sin of all humanity, for Adam was the head of all humanity. If he had been faithful, we would have enjoyed all of his gifts, for he acted in our name. Since he was unfaithful, we suffer his loss, for he acted in our name. This is not an injustice. All human beings are bound up with one another. In 1917, for example, President Wilson proclaimed war without any explicit declaration on the part of any of us. He was our political head and he acted in our name. Adam was our head, and he acted in our name. When he declared war against God, we declared war in like manner, without any explicit declaration on our part, because of our oneness with him. And just as in the physical order the infected blood of a father may pass on to a son, so too the stain of the first man has passed on to the whole human race and stained everyone but our "tainted nature's solitary boast" — the Blessed Mother of our Lord and Savior Jesus Christ.

Finally, original sin alone can explain the almost contradictory character of human nature which makes a man aspire to higher things and at the same time succumb to the baser. The only reason we ever seek the nobler things of God is that we once possessed them; we seek because once we found.

All religion is full of a sense of uneasiness and need of deliverance; every great student of human nature has echoed as true the words of the great

Latin poet Ovid, who testified that we all approve the better things, but often follow the worse; all peoples and nations have put their golden age in the past, when the chosen ones of their race once walked with God. What is this universal testimony of humanity but the witness to the fact of original sin? Our lives are like the great unfinished Gothic cathedrals of Europe, ever testifying that our ideals are never completely realized here below. The conjectures of anthropologists about primitive man are nothing compared to the solid fact of the sense of human sin. By its nature, the evidence of Eden is something we cannot find. By its nature the evidence of sin is something one cannot help finding. As a matter of personal experience something has happened — we are not what we ought to be.

There are ultimately only two possible theories to account for the nature and the origin of man: one is that the life of man is a push from below; the other, that the life of man is a gift from above; the one is that man is wholly of the earth, earthly; the other, that he is partly of the heavens, heavenly. The second is the Christian conception: man is not a risen beast, he is rather a kind of fallen angel. His origin is hidden not in the slime and dust of prehistoric forests, but in the clear daylight of paradise where he communed with God; his origin looks back not to cosmic forces, but to divine grace. On this conception man is supposed to act not like a beast because he came from one, but like God because he was made to His own image and likeness.

The assertion is often made today that man became the beauty of the world and the paragon of animals either because he lost the hand of a beast or the foot of an animal or the visage of an orangutan. No, man is what he is because of the immortal soul breathed into him by God. Let a man keep the hand of a beast, but give him an immortal soul, and it will not be long until he will be moving that hand over the keys of a piano and drawing out of it the melodies of a Mozart. Let a man keep the lips of a gibbon, but give him an immortal soul, and it will not be long until those lips will not be muttering vague cries in the dark, but calling to honest men, as Demosthenes did in the marketplace of Athens. Let him even keep the tail of a beast, but give him an immortal soul, and it will not be long until that tail will be picking up a pen and writing dramas like those of Sophocles and poetry like that of Dante. It is not the physical that makes man what he is, but the divine; it is not the loss of something animal-like that will make something Godlike out of man. The greatness of man is not so much his emergence from animality as his ascent into deity, and the power that wrought such greatness is not so much an ascent from below as a descent from above in which the infinite heart of a God calls out in the heart of a babe.

Which of these two views of man is nobler?

The one regards him as a little biochemical entity of flesh and blood, not more than six feet tall, apt to be killed by a microbe; standing self-poised and self-centered in such a universe as this, acknowledging in self-conceit no God, no purpose, no future, and still hoping that the blind cosmic forces of space and time will sweep him on until he becomes lost in the bursting of the great cosmic bubble. The other shows us that same being awakened to his own actual ignorance, his possible wisdom; his own actual sinfulness, his possible saintliness; his own actual humanity, his possible sharing in the life of Christ; and then by an act of self-distrust which is the highest kind of self-assertion, enrolling himself under no less a person than the Son of God made Man and crying out directly to the Lord of the universe, "I am yours, O God. O help me whom You have made."

When a man answers this question aright, he will understand something of the true nature of man and the love of God who came to restore the gifts which man had lost, and in gratitude his heart will cry out:

> "My God! My God! What is a heart,
> that Thou shouldst it so eye and woo,
> pouring upon it all Thy art,
> as if Thou hadst nothing else to do?"

GOD'S QUEST FOR MAN

God's Quest For Man

Love is naturally expansive, but Divine Love is creative. Love told the secret of its goodness to nothingness, and that was creation. Love made something like unto its own image and likeness, and that was man. Love is prodigal of its gifts, and that was the elevation of man to the adoptive sonship of God. Love must always run risks of not being loved in return, for love is free. The human heart refused to return that love in the only way in which love can ever be shown, namely by confidence and trust in a moment of trial. Man thus lost the gifts of God, darkened his intellect, weakened his will, and brought the first or original sin into the world, for sin is ultimately a refusal to love.

It was the refusal of man to love the best that created the most difficult problem in the whole history of humanity, namely the problem of restoring man to the favor of Divine Love. In short, the problem was this: Man had sinned; but his sin was not merely a rebellion against another man, but a revolt against the infinite love of God. Therefore his sin was infinite. But, it may be asked, since man is finite, how can he commit an infinite crime? The answer to that question is that an offense, an injury, or a sin is always to be measured by the one sinned against. It would be, for example, a far greater offense to insult the mayor of a city than a citizen of that city, and it would be a greater offense to commit a crime against the governor of the state than against the mayor. In like manner, it would be a still greater offense to commit a felony against the President of the United States than against the governor of any state. In other words, sin is measured by the one sinned against. Man sinned against God. God is infinite. Therefore, man's offense is infinite.

Such is one side of the problem. The other side is this: Every infraction or violation of a law demands reparation or atonement. We need only go into the hospitals to see that every violation of a law of nature has its reckoning day; we need only go into our asylums to see that nature itself takes revenge on excesses, and squares her accounts with sin. A judge seems to be sitting there in judgment executing sentence upon those who would violate her commands. In a still higher sphere parents who love their children demand reparation for their faults, and judges who love society impose sentences in atonement for crime; for a justice which sees evil and does not punish it, is not justice. Since God is infinite love, he might pardon man and forget the injury, but pardon without compensation would eclipse the justice which is the nature of God. Without setting any limits to the mercy of God, I could understand His action better if His mercy was preceded by a satisfaction for sin, for one can never be merciful unless he is just. Mercy is the overflow of justice.

But assuming that man should give satisfaction, could he satisfy adequately for his sin? No, because the satisfaction or reparation or atonement which man had to offer was only finite. At this point it may be asked: Why cannot man give an infinite recompense for his sin? If he can commit an infinite crime, why can he not make an infinite retribution? The answer is that while injury is in the one injured, honor or reparation is in the one honoring. If a citizen of the Soviet Union, a Minister of Finance of France, a Senator of a South American country, and the Queen of Great Britain came to call on the President of our country, they would not all render him equal honor. Honor would be in the one honoring and he who held the highest office would render the greatest tribute. Now I have said that man owes honor and reparation to God; but since man is finite, it follows that the honor which he will render to God would also be finite. And there is the problem of the Incarnation.

Man, who is finite, owes an infinite debt. But how can a man who owes a million pay the debt with a cent? How can the human atone to the divine? How can justice and mercy be reconciled? If satisfaction is ever to be made for the fall of man, the finite and the infinite, the human and the divine, God and man must in some way be linked together. It would not do for God alone to come down and suffer as God alone, for then He would not have anything in common with man; the sin was not God's, but man's. It would not do for man alone to suffer or atone, for the merit of his sufferings would be only finite. If the satisfaction were to be complete, two conditions would have to be fulfilled: First, man would have to be man to act as man and to atone. Man would have to be God in order that his sufferings should have an infinite value. But in order that the finite and the infinite should not be acting as two distinct personalities, and in order that infinite merit should result from man's suffering, God and man in some way would have to become one, or in other words, there would have to be a God-man. If justice and mercy were to be reconciled, there would have to be an Incarnation, which means God assuming a human nature in such a way that he would be true God and true man. There would have to be a union of God and man, built upon somewhat the same lines as the union of spirit and matter in man. Man has a double nature, the nature of a body which is material, the nature of the soul which is spiritual, and yet he is only one person. The Incarnation of God would imply some such union of two natures in the unity of a person, but quite naturally a far more perfect one.

Let me make this solution clear by an example. On the desk before me is a pencil. That pencil represents human nature; of itself the pencil cannot write. My hand now goes down to the pencil, takes it up, moves it across a paper, and immediately the pencil is endowed with a power which before it had not. If after I had written, you should ask me who wrote the lines, I would not say my fingers wrote them, nor would I say my pencil wrote them, but I would say, I wrote them. In other words, we attribute the actions of various natures to a person and the one thing that characterizes the person is not action, not nature, not direction, but responsibility. That is why I do not say my stomach is hungry, but I am hungry; not my eyes see, but I see. Actions belong to the person.

Now let the pencil represent poor human nature, of itself unable to pay an infinite debt to God. Imagine now a divine person with a divine nature coming down to that human nature, taking it up and becoming united with it in a far more perfect way than my hand is united with the pencil. If such an act of condescension should ever happen, the action of the human nature and the action of the divine nature would not be attributed to either nature alone, as the action of the pencil would not be attributed to the nature of the pencil or to the nature of the hand alone; it would be attributed to the person. But if the person were one of the Persons of the Blessed

Trinity, namely, the second Person, the eternal Son of God, it would follow that every thought, every word, every sigh, every tear of the human nature of that person would be the very thought, very word, very sigh, and very tear of God. Then justice and mercy could be reconciled. God would be just in demanding infinite satisfaction; God would be merciful in making that possible by coming down to earth and being found in the habit and the form of man.

What I have just imagined for you is what has actually taken place. Love tends to become like the one loved; in fact, it even wishes to become one with the one loved. God loved unworthy man. He willed to become one with him, and that was the Incarnation. One night there went out over the stillness of an evening breeze, out over the white chalked hills of Bethlehem, a cry, a gentle cry. The sea did not hear the cry, for the sea was filled with its own voice. The earth did not hear the cry, for the earth slept. The great men of the earth did not hear the cry, for they could not understand how a child could be greater than a man. The kings of the earth did not hear the cry, for they could not fathom how a king could be born in a stable. There were only two classes of men who heard the cry that night: shepherds and wise men. Shepherds: those who know they know nothing. Wise men: those who know they do not know everything. Shepherds: poor simple men who knew only how to tend their flocks, who perhaps could not tell who was the governor of Judea; who, perhaps, did not know a single line of Virgil, though there was not a Roman who could not quote from him. On the other hand, there were the wise men; not kings, but teachers of kings; men who knew how to read the stars, to tell the story of their movements; men who were constantly bent on discovery. Both of these heard the cry. The shepherds found their Shepherd, and the wise men discovered Wisdom. And the Shepherd and Wisdom was a Babe in a crib.

And from that day to this there have been only two classes of people who have heard the cry of Christ and who have found Christ: the very simple and the very learned. The very simple — good souls who know perhaps only how to tell their beads, and the very wise minds like Pascal, Aquinas, Bonaventure, and Mercier. But never the man who thinks he knows. Only the simple and only the wise find Christ, because both are humble; both acknowledge either ignorance or the limitations of human knowledge, which is humility. In order to enter the cave, one must stoop; and the stoop is the stoop of humility. Those who possess that kind of humility can enter the cave. There they will find what these two groups have found: a Babe outstretched on a bed of straw. So great was the majesty seated on the brow of the Child, so great was the dignity of the Babe, so powerful was the light of those eyes that shone like two celestial suns, that they could not help but cry out: "Emmanuel: God is with us." God revealed Himself to man again. He who is born without a mother in heaven is born without a father on earth. He who made His mother is born of His mother. He who made all flesh is born of flesh. "The bird that built the nest is hatched therein." Maker of the sun, under the sun; Molder of the earth, on the earth; ineffably wise, a little infant; filling the world, lying in a manger; ruling the stars, suckling a breast; the mirth of heaven weeps; God becomes man; Creator, a creature. Rich becomes poor; Divinity, incarnate; Majesty, subjugated; Liberty, captive; Eternity, time; Master, a servant; Truth, accused; Judge, judged; Justice, condemned; Lord, scourged; Power, bound with ropes; King, crowned with thorns; Salvation, wounded; Life, dead. "The eternal Word is dumb." Marvel of marvels! Union of unions! Three mysterious unions in one; divinity and humanity; virginity and fecundity; faith and the heart of man. And though we shall live on through eternity, eternity will not be long enough for us to understand the mystery of that "Child who was a father and of the mother who was a child."

The tiny hands that were not quite long enough to touch the huge heads of the cattle, were the hands that were holding the reins that steer the sun, the moon, and the stars in their courses. The tiny fingers that could but clutch clumsily at the coarse straw of the threshing floor were fingers that will one day point in judgment to the good and to the bad. The tiny feet that could not walk were weak, not because they were baby feet, but because those baby feet could not bear the weight of divine omnipotence. There under the tender skin of a baby brow was beating an intelligence compared to which the combined intelligences of Europe and America amount to naught; an intelligence that, if it had moved in other days, would have found Plato and Aristotle but poor philosophers, Dante and Shakespeare but poor poets, and our modern scientists but mumbling beginners. Each breath, each sigh, and each tear of that babe was the breath, sigh, and tear of God. Each one of them would have been sufficient to have redeemed ten thousand worlds. Then why a life of suffering and why an existence that led to the hard bed of the cross? Why the shedding of the last drop of blood? For something like the same reason that there are more birds than are necessary for the needed song of man, more grains of sand than are necessary for a seashore — because of the superfluity of love. Love which is real loves even to the point of sacrifice, in fact loves even to the end which is the giving of one's own life. Christ loves to that extent, for "Greater love than this no man has, that a man lay down his life for his friends."

The drying of the blood of Christ on an infamous gibbet, then, is something more than some in our day would have us believe, who declare that Christ's death is interesting and valuable because of the subjective effect it has on the mind of the believer. He went to death, they tell us, in order that man might be impressed with His heroism. No! He went to death not to impress us subjectively, but to save us objectively. Imagine a man sitting on a pier on a bright sunny day, lazily fishing and apparently without a concern in the world. Now suppose that a stranger wishing to impress that fisherman with the great humanitarian love he bore him, would rush forward, cast himself headlong over the pier into the sea, and drown. The whole matter would be ridiculous, for there is no relation between the fisherman's need and the act of the benefactor. But suppose the fisherman had fallen into the water and was drowning. Then the friend came and threw himself in to save him and gave his own life in the rescue; in such a case we would say: "Greater love than this no man has, that a man lay down his life for his friends." Here there is an objective relation between the man's need and the rescue; so, too, in the greater drama of salvation there is a relation between man who was lost in sin, and God who came to save him — not by gold or silver, but by the outpouring of His precious blood. And if you were the only person in the world who ever lived, He would have come down and suffered and died just for you alone. That is how much God loves you.

It takes a divine, an infinite Being to use the very instruments of defeat as the instruments of victory. The fall came through three realities: first, a disobedient man, Adam; second, a proud woman, Eve; third, a tree. The reconciliation and redemption of man came through these same three. For the disobedient man, Adam, was the obedient new Adam of the human race, Christ; for the proud Eve, there was the humble Mary; and for the tree, the cross.

In the face of this cardinal doctrine of Christianity, which is the Incarnation of God, how tawdry and poor appear the substitutes offered in which we are asked to venerate a system, prostrate ourselves before a series of abstract nouns or fall down on our knees before the cosmos. These things are too unreal, for the very reason that they are systems and hence will never appeal to the heart of man. Humanism is impossible because it is too academic; love of humanity is impossible because there is no such thing as humanity — there are only men and women; the religion of progress is impossible because progress means nothing unless we know whither we are progressing. Philosophical systems, scientific constructions, and slogans leave the heart of man cold. Even a theory about love means little as long as it remains a theory. But let love become personal in someone and then it pulls at every heartstring in the world. There is the secret of the appeal of the

Incarnation. Love became Incarnate and dwelt among us. Since that day hearts that have known what the Incarnation means can never content themselves with any system which asks us to adore the cosmos. Man never has loved, never will love anything he cannot get his arms around, and the cosmos is too big and too bulky. *That is why the immense God became a Babe in order that we might encircle Him in our arms.*

THE DIVINE EQUATION

The Divine Equation

Love tends to become one with the one loved: this was the Incarnation in which God became man. Love knows no limits in its giving: this was the redemption through the merits of Jesus Christ, accomplished through the person of God taking upon Himself a human nature, like ours in all things except sin. Thus far we have progressed in our unfolding of the Divine Romance.

Now we go on to inquire: What did Christ do with the human nature which He assumed and united to His divine person? What did He do with that body which He took from the Blessed Mother Mary, and which in its physical state lived from the crib to the cross? He did many things with it, but they are all reducible to three: He *taught*, He *governed*, and He *sanctified*.

First, He taught, not as the scribes and Pharisees, but as one having authority. Conscious that He was the eternal Word of God that illumined every man coming into the world, He taught not as a searcher of truth but as one communicating it from its very source and fountainhead: "I am the Truth."

Desiring that others should share in that truth, He gathered men about Him and bade them go out and teach the nations of the earth to observe all things whatsoever He had commanded.

Second, He used his body not only to teach but also to govern and to found a kingdom. All government is based upon power. Conscious of His union with His heavenly Father, He could say: "All power is given to Me in heaven and on earth." Gathering the elements of His first kingdom, consisting mostly of ignorant men, He chose from the twelve of them one as their chief and guide — Peter the Rock, on whom He said He would build His Church, and to whom He committed the supreme power of feeding His lambs and feeding His sheep.

Thirdly, with His body He sanctified: "I have come that you may have life and have it in abundance." Through the instrumentality of that body He opened blind eyes to the light of God's sunshine, unstopped deaf ears to the music of the human voice, forgave penitent Magdalene, sanctified the woman at the well, and remade Nicodemus as one born anew. But as He sent out His apostles to teach His truth, to establish the government of His kingdom, He now sends them out as His Father had sent Him, to forgive sins, to cast out devils, and to renew His sacrifice in commemoration of Him, and to baptize in the name of the Father and of the Son and of the Holy Spirit.

In other words, the human nature or the body of our Blessed Lord was the conjoined instrument by which He taught, governed, and sanctified; by it He communicated His *truth* as teacher, His *law* as king, and His *life* as a priest, for He was the Truth, the Way and the Life.

The remarkable thing about His earthly life was the fact that He often spoke of it continuing after His death, for He who laid down His life could take it up again. He reminded His apostles over and over again that after His Resurrection He would assume another body, not a body like the one which He took from the Blessed Mother, but rather a kind of social body which would be made up of all those who became incorporated into His kingdom. He said that this union between Himself and this body would be organic, vital and lifelike, like a union of the vine and the branches, and just as the branches could not live without the vine, so neither could this new body of His live without Him. He promised them that He would not leave them orphans, but that He would remain with them all days even to the consummation of the world, and that when two or more were gathered together in His name He would be in the midst of them. Finally, He told them that He would become so much identified with the poor, hungry, persecuted members of this new body, that whoever should do a kindness to any member of that body, or even so much as give him a drink, would be doing it unto Him; that this body would not be like an institution, but like a mustard seed that would grow from small beginnings to fill the whole earth, and that between it and Himself there would be something of the unity that existed between Him and His heavenly Father — "I in You and You in Me."

He did say, however, that His union with this new body would not be complete until the day of Pentecost, for He would not "assume" His new mystical body until He had taken His own physical body from this earth. He left the elements of this new body, namely, His apostles, on earth when He ascended into heaven. But this little group of men gathered about Him were as yet wanting a soul for their corporate unity, fighting as they were for first place in the kingdom of heaven, and even returning to their nets and their boats after the Resurrection. They were like the chemicals that exist in a laboratory, which chemicals could make up the physical constituents of a body and yet cannot combine to make a body because they lack a soul or vivifying spirit. They were as yet a kind of organization; but they were to become an organism under the influence of the Spirit of Christ that would come on Pentecost. Ten days after the Ascension of our Blessed Lord into heaven, the Holy Spirit descended upon the apostles gathered in the upper room of Jerusalem, baptized them with fire, gave them a soul, made them one, signed them with a sign and sealed them with a seal; and at that precise moment the new body of Christ was born — the body of Christ is His Church. In the fiery glow of that Pentecostal gift, the small and scattered rays combined to form one great radiance, and they who before had been but men of little faith, filled with childish egotism, now went into the world conscious that they were the beginning of that new body of Christ which would grow as the mustard seed even to the consummation of the world.

Am I teaching a strange and novel doctrine when I say that the Church is the body of Christ? Recall to your mind an incident that happened within twenty years after the day of Pentecost, within which time that new body of Christ had grown and expanded to fill much of the then known world. The incident that I refer to is that of Saul of Tarsus, the fiery Hebrew of the Hebrews, who hated Christ and things Christian as much as any man could hate. Armed with letters from the synagogue of Jerusalem, he set out for the city of Damascus to seize and persecute the Christians there who belonged to the Church or the body of Christ. While he was on the way, suddenly a great light shone round about him. He fell to the ground and heard a voice saying to him: "Saul, Saul, why are you persecuting Me?" The heat of the Oriental sun gave him strength to speak, and nothingness dared ask the name of Omnipotence: "Who are you, Lord?" The answer came back: "I am Jesus whom you are persecuting." Saul was persecuting the Church of Damascus and the Christians of Damascus, and Christ said to Saul: "Why are you persecuting Me?" Christ and the Church, are they the same thing? Precisely! The Church is Christ and Christ is the Church — such is the divine equation.

Saul learned the unforgettable lesson that day which he afterwards taught as Paul: the lesson which Christ Himself had taught to His apostles, the lesson which is taught to us now, namely, that the Church is the body of Christ, and that Christ Himself sitting at the right hand of the Father is the Head of that body. This new body, sometimes called a mystical body, is to be understood after the analogy of the human body which is made up of many members performing different functions and yet all cooperating toward the harmony of the whole. The hand is not the foot, the eye is not the ear, the heart is not the lung. So, too, the priest is not the layman, the apostle is not the disciple, the Vicar of Christ is not the deacon, and yet all are one in the same Spirit. As St. Paul puts it, "For as in one body we have many members, but all the members do not have the same function, so we, though many, are one body in Christ, and individually members of one another."

The Church, then, in the language of Sacred Scripture is the body of Christ, not the physical one like the one that was born in Bethlehem and was crucified in Jerusalem, but rather a mystical one in which He continues to live and to act and to think (though in another sense than He did in Judea and Galilee). And He, Christ in heaven, is the Head of that body. As He took a body from Mary, who was filled with the Holy Spirit, with which He lived a physical life of thirty-three years, so He lives today His mystical life in a new body taken from humanity but likewise overshadowed with the Pentecostal Spirit, which we call the Church. As His Incarnation was made up of a visible and an invisible element, a human and a divine; so, too, His continued incarnation in His Church is made up of two elements, one human and the other divine. The human element in it is poor, weak humanity, and the divine element is the life of God. With this new body taken from humanity and filled with His Spirit, Christ is reliving His life at Bethlehem, Nazareth, Galilee, and Jerusalem. He is doing with this new body three things, as He did three things with His physical body: with it He teaches, He governs and He sanctifies.

First of all, He teaches. But how does He teach? He who is invisible teaches through the instrumentality of His body. A teacher in a classroom, for example, wishes to communicate a spiritual truth, such as love of duty. That spiritual truth is something which has no matter, no size, no weight or color, and yet it is communicated materially by writing, by words, or by examples. It does not become a different truth when it is communicated visibly or audibly; so, neither is the truth which is taught by the visible head of His mystical body, who is His Vicar on earth, a truth different from the truth of Christ. Just as His own physical body had a visible head, so, too, His mystical body has a visible head. This visible head is the successor of His first Vicar on whom He built His Church, promising that the gates of hell would not prevail against it. Two conclusions follow: The first is, that the truth which is communicated to the body through its visible head, the Vicar of Christ, is not a spiritual truth distinct from the truth existing in the invisible head of the Church, which is Christ Himself, any more than the spiritual truth of the teacher became another truth when articulated. The truth of Christ and the truth of His Vicar are one and the same, and such is the meaning of the words: "He who hears you, hears Me." The second is that the truth will be necessarily infallible, or free from error, for it is essentially the truth of Christ, and hence the infallibility of the Vicar of Christ is only another way of saying the infallibility of Christ. Infallibility is an endowment of the body with which its visible head thinks and speaks the mind of Christ. And to deny that Christ can communicate His truth as He communicated it centuries ago is to limit the truth of the Son of God to Palestine as a space and to thirty-three years as a time. To the members of that body Christ speaks through the Peter of our own day as He spoke through the Peter of the first.

Second, Christ not only teaches through the instrumentality of His body, which is the Church, but He also governs through it. The supreme legislative, executive, and judicial decisions of the Vicar and those under his authority are the decisions of Christ and therefore binding with the authority of Christ. My will, for example, may direct that my hand be moved. The decision of my will is invisible, but the manifestations of my will are external and visible. So, too, the will of Christ and the government of His Church are expressed through the visible head of His body and those joined to him as the other apostles were joined to Peter. This alone gives the key to the child-like obedience so incomprehensible to the outsider which we give to the Church, an obedience whereby we submit to it as the will of Christ expressed in the action of His Vicar. It is for us no slave mentality, no corpse-like servitude, but a profoundly religious act, an absolute devotion to Christ paid by His children who are enjoying the glorious liberty of the children of God.

Finally, Christ does a third thing with His body: He sanctifies with it. The body of Christ is continually receiving through seven mysterious physical signs, the energy of divine life. Through the instrumentality of bread, water, oil, and human speech the very life of Christ Himself is poured into the very cells of the mystical body, which we are. To each person is permitted a liberal handling of His precious wounds. Each sacrament is a kiss of God, a material thing used as a means of spiritual sanctification, and the true minister of every sacrament is none other than the supreme and eternal High Priest — Christ Himself.

In summary, then, Christ who in His human body taught, governed, and sanctified, now continues to do the same in His mystical body, and her teachings are Christ's infallible teachings; her commands, Christ's divine commands; and her sacramental life, Christ's divine life. The Church, then, is the continuation of the Incarnation. It is not an institution like a bank, but a life; not an organization like a club, but an organism; not something *horizontal* extending from the apostles as men to us as other men, but as something *vertical* in which divine life descends first from God to Christ, and then on to us in the Church.

The Gospel therefore is being re-lived by the presence of Christ in His new body, which is the Church. Just as His own human body was subject to physical weaknesses, just as it became tired at Jacob's well, and had its lips blistered with the kiss of Judas, so I see His own mystical body subject not to physical weakness, but to moral weakness and scandals, and even to other betraying lips. But I can see no more reason for doubting the divinity of His mystical body because of its failures and weaknesses, than I can see a reason for doubting the divinity of Christ because three of His apostles slept in the garden.

Through the lips of the Church I hear Christ speaking, and her words I accept as the very words of Christ. When she lifts her hands in the confessional and bids the sinner go and sin no more, I see once more Christ lifting His hands in forgiveness as onlookers taunt Him: "How can man forgive sins?" When I see some of her own children leave her because they cannot accept her doctrine, I see Christ once more permitting His own chosen disciples who found His sayings hard, to leave Him and walk with Him no more. When I see her hold aloft a white host in the chalice and say to me: "Behold the Lamb of God," I believe that Christ Himself is as really and truly there as if He should throw open the tabernacle door and declare unto me His living presence. When I see a priest mount the altar steps to renew the sacrifice of Calvary, I see once more the bleeding feet of Christ climbing the hill and His wounded hands outstretched on the gibbet of a cross. When I hear her call men and women away from the lights and glamours of the world to the shades and shadows of the cross where saints are made, I hear once more Christ commending Mary because she had chosen the better part, and I know that, after all, only one thing in life is necessary and that is the salvation of a soul. When I hear her misunderstood and hated by the world, I can hear Christ once more reminding us: "Because I have taken you out of the world, therefore the world will hate you. But remember that it has hated Me before you."

In those moments when she is accused of being unscientific, behind the times, and the Church of the poor, I hear men once more asking Christ: "Can anything good come out of Nazareth?" In those other moments when the world shouts and acclaims her and would almost crown her king, I see the palm branches of triumph change into spears of threat. Then in those moments of sorrow when the Church goes on trial and I hear her condemned for being too undogmatic, I am reminded of Annas' complaint that Christ would not speak out concerning His ministry and His doctrine. When I hear her condemned because she is too dogmatic in asserting her divinity, I am reminded of Christ being condemned by Caiaphas because He was too outspoken about His divinity. When I hear her charged with being too worldly and unpatriotic, I take the charges merely as echoes made before Pilate's palace that Christ was perverting the nation and refusing to give tribute to Caesar. When I hear her condemned for being too unworldly and refusing to compromise, I can almost see Herod once again robing Christ in the garment of a fool because He would not do a worldly trick to gain His release. When the charges are added, viz., that she is too dogmatic or too undogmatic, too worldly or too unworldly, I recall that they are contradictory charges and that the only fitting punishment for one condemned on contradictory charges is the sign of contradiction: the cross on which one bar is at variance and in contradiction with the other.

The Church, then, must have her passion days even as Christ, and must be condemned in three languages, in Hebrew, Latin, and Greek, in the cultures of Jerusalem, Rome, and Athens, in the name of the good, the true, and the beautiful. Now as then the representatives of these three cultures pass beneath the cross and ask that the Church give up and come down. Those who crucify in the name of the good, shout unto her: "Come down from your belief in the spiritual destiny of man; come down from your belief that man has been made to the image and likeness of God; come down from your belief in the sanctity of marriage, come down and we will believe." Those who crucify in the name of the true, pass beneath the cross and plead: "Come down from your belief that there is such a thing as truth; come down from your belief in the divinity of Christ and the existence of God; come down from your belief in the continued life and truth of Christ in His Church. Can you not see that there are other crosses on Calvary beside your own? Come down and we will believe." Those who crucify in the name of the beautiful shout: "Come down from your belief that salvation is purchased through mortification; come down from your belief that the only way to save a life is to lose it; come down from your belief that another world is to be purchased by the tempered enjoyment of this one! See the straits to which your philosophy has already led you. Your flesh is hanging like purple rags. Come down and we will believe."

The divinely supreme miracle of Christ's whole life and the whole life of the Church is that she does not come down. The miracle of the crucifixion is the fact that Christ still hangs there. Divinity in such moments is shown by restraint of power. A human being would have stepped down with the same impetuousness with which weak men answer timid challenges. The miracle is to be able to come down, and yet not to come down. It is human to come down, but it is divine to hang there. It would be easy for the Church to come down; to have been Gnostic in the first century, to have been Arian in the fourth, and to be pagan in the twentieth. It is always easy to let the age have its head, but it is difficult to keep one's own. It is always easy to fall; there are a thousand angles at which a thing will fall but only one at which it stands, and that is the angle at which the Church is poised between heaven and earth. From that angle she overlooks the passing fads and fancies of the ages, and sings over them in deep and sonorous tones a requiem in the languages of Hebrew, Latin, and Greek, awaiting the day when she shall come down to walk in the glory of her new Easter morn.

THE PULPIT OF THE CROSS

The Pulpit of the Cross

Our Blessed Lord during His mortal life chose many varied and picturesque pulpits from which to deliver His sermons — the words of eternal life. Sometimes His pulpit was Peter's bark pushed out into the sea. At other times, it was the crowded streets of Jericho; on another occasion, the Golden Gate of the Temple, and on still another, Jacob's well. It seemed as if almost any pulpit pleased Him, until the day came for Him to deliver His last and farewell address to the world. Then He would not be content with any pulpit; then He would demand a pulpit which, like the words He was uttering, would be remembered down through the arches of the years. And on that Good Friday morning, as He stood on the sunlit portico of Pontius Pilate, perhaps he thought of making that portico the pulpit of His last and farewell address to the world. There was a vast sea of faces before Him and hearts hungering for the bread of eternal life; there was an audience that anyone would have loved to have opened His heart. But no, He would not make that portico the pulpit of His last and farewell address. He would wait for a few hours, for another pulpit which would be given Him at the foot of the steps of Pilate's palace; and that pulpit He would put upon His shoulders and carry to Golgotha, for it would be—the cross.

Once on those heights He offered Himself to his executioners. Hands of the carpenter hardened by toil; hands from which the world's graces flow; feet of the miracle worker that went about doing good and that trod the everlasting hills, now had the rough nails applied to them. The first knock of the hammer is heard in silence; blow follows blow and is faintly reechoed over the city walls beneath. Mary and John hold their ears. The sound is unendurable; each echo sounds as another stroke. The cross is lifted slowly off the ground, staggers for a moment in midair, and then, with a thud that seemed to shake even hell itself, it sank into the pit prepared for it. Our Blessed Lord has mounted His pulpit for the last time, and what a majestic pulpit it is! In itself the cross is a sermon. How much more eloquently it speaks now when adorned with the Word of eternal life!

Like all who mount their pulpits, He overlooked His audience. Far off in the distance, down over the Valley of Jehoshaphat, and over on the other side of the valley, He could see the gilded roof of the Temple reflecting its rays against the sun, which was soon to hide its face in shame. Here and there on Temple walls He caught glimpses of figures straining their eyes to catch the last view of Him whom the darkness knew not. Nearer the pulpit, but off at the border of the crowd, stood some of His own timid disciples ready to flee in case of danger. Greeks and Romans were there, too, as well as scribes and Pharisees from Jerusalem. There were Temple priests in the crowd asking Him to come down and prove His divinity. There were the Deity-blind, mocking and spitting at Him. There were some who had followed Him for an hour, taunting Him, saying that others He had saved, but Himself He could not save. There were Roman soldiers throwing dice for the garments of God. And there at the foot of the cross stood that wounded flower, that broken thing, Magdalene, forgiven because she loved much. And there, with a face like a cast molded out of love, was John. And there, God pity her! was His own mother, Mary. Mary, Magdalene and John; Innocence, Penitence and Priesthood: the three types of souls forever to be found beneath the cross of Christ.

All is silence now. The scribes and Pharisees cease their raillery, the Roman soldiers put away their dice. The sky is darkened, and men grow fearful. They are awaiting the farewell address of the Son of God. He begins to speak, but like all men who die, He thinks of those whom He loves most. His first word was a word about His enemies: "Father, forgive them, for they know not what they do." His second word was about sinners, and He spoke to a

thief: "This day you will be with Me in paradise."
And the thief died a thief, for he stole paradise! His
third word was to His saints. It was the new annun-
ciation: "Mother, behold your son." As the sermon
went on, it seemed to gain in emphasis about the
love of God for man and at this particular point that
we are now considering, when He began to speak, it
was not a curse upon those who crucified Him; it
was not a word of reproach to the timid disciples off
at the border of the crowd; it was not a word of
withering scorn to those who taunted and mocked
Him; it was not a proud prophetic word of power to
those who chided His weakness; it was not a word
of hate to the Roman soldiers; it was not a word of
hope to Magdalene; it was not a word of love to John;
it was not a word of farewell to His own mother; it
was not even to God at this moment, it was to man!
And out from the abundance of the Sacred Heart
there welled the cry of cries: "I thirst."

He, the God-man! He who holds the earth in
the palm of His hand, He from whose fingertips have
tumbled planets and worlds, He who threw the stars
into their orbits, and spheres into space, now asks
man, a piece of His own handiwork, to help Him! He
asks man for a drink! Not a drink of earthly water,
that is not what He wanted, but a drink of love — I
thirst for love.

There is perhaps no word in the English language that is more often used and more often

misunderstood than the word that rang out from the pulpit of the cross on that day: the simple word, *love*. Love as the world understands it means to have, to own, to possess: to have that object, to own that thing, to possess that person, for the particular pleasure which it will give. That is not love; that is selfishness, that is sin. Love is not the desire to have, to own, to possess. Love is the desire to be had, to be owned, to be possessed. Love is the giving of oneself for the sake of another. Love, as the world understands it, is symbolized by a circle which is always circumscribed by self. Love, as our Lord understands it, is symbolized by the cross with its arms outstretched even unto infinity to embrace all humanity within its grasp. As long as we have a body, then, love can never mean anything else but sacrifice. That is why we speak of "arrows" and "darts" of love — something that wounds.

But if love, in its highest reaches, means sacrifice, then these words of our Blessed Lord from the cross are the climax of Love's ways with unloving men. Love did not keep the secret of its goodness — that was creation. Love became one with the one loved, and that was the Incarnation. But if Love had merely stopped with God becoming man, we might say that God did not do everything He could do to show His love; we might say that He was like the heathen gods that sat indifferent to the woes and ills and heartaches of the world and hence never drew from the heart of man a beat of love. If divine Love stopped merely by appearing among us, man might say that God could never understand the sufferings of the loneliness of a human heart; that God could not love as men do, namely, to the point of sacrifice. If, therefore, Love was to give of its fullness, it must express itself to the point of sacrificing itself for the salvation and redemption of mankind. If, therefore, He who suffered on Calvary, He who was now preaching from the pulpit of the cross, were not God, but a mere creature or a mere man, then there must be creatures in this world better and nobler than God. Shall man who toils for his fellow man, suffers for him, and if need be dies for him, be capable of doing that which God cannot do? Should this noblest form of love, which is sacrifice, be possible to sinful man, and yet impossible to a perfectly good God? Shall we say that the martyr sprinkling the sands of the Colosseum with his blood, the soldier dying for his country, the missionary spending himself and being spent for the good of heathens; aye, and more, shall we say that those women, martyrs by pain, who in little hovels and lowly cottages have sacrificed all the joys of life for the sake of simple duties, and little charities, unnoticed and unknown by all save God — shall we say that all those, who from the beginning of the world have shown forth the beauty of sacrifice, have no divine prototype in heaven? That they have been capable of displaying a nobler form of love than He who made them? That they have shown greater love than Love itself? Shall we say this, or shall we say with John and Paul, that if man can be so good, God must be infinitely better; that if man can love so much, God can love infinitely more? Shall we not say this, and find in the cross of Calvary the perfect expression of love by an all-perfect being, of whom perfect condescension and sacrifice were required by naught in heaven or on earth save by His own perfect and inconceivable love which He now preaches from the pulpit of the cross? If we do say this, that he is very God of God, and that love is now reaching its climax in the redemption of mankind, then no longer can men say, "Why does God send men into the world to be miserable when He is happy?" — for the God-man is miserable now. No longer can men say, "God makes me suffer pain while He goes through none," for the God-man is now enduring pain to the utmost. No longer can men say that God has a heart that cannot under-stand, for now His own Sacred Heart understands what it is to be abandoned by God and man as He suffers suspended between the kingdoms of both, between heaven and earth, rejected by one and abandoned by the other. Now it is true to say of Love Itself that it is really dying for us, for "Greater love than this no man has, that a man lay down his life for his friends."

The drama of that day is an abiding one. For Calvary is not just a mere historical incident, like the battle of Waterloo; it is not something which has happened, it is something which is also happening. Christ is still on the cross.

> "Whenever there is silence around me
> By day or by night —
> I am startled by a cry.
> It came down from the cross —
> The first time I heard it.
> I went out and searched —
> And found a man in the throes of crucifixion
> And I said, 'I will take you down,'
> And I tried to take the nails out of his feet.
> But he said, 'Let them be
> For I cannot be taken down
> Until every man, every woman, and every child
> Come together to take me down.'
> And I said, 'But I cannot bear your cry.
> What can I do?'
> And he said, 'Go, about the world —
> Tell everyone that you meet —
> That there is a man on the cross.'"

Because of sin Christ dies again, for as St. Paul reminds us, as often as we sin we "crucify again to ourselves the Son of God." The scars are still open. "Earth's pain still stands deified," and still like falling stars Christ's blood-drops crimson the robes of other Johns and the hair of other Magdalenes. As long as earth wears wounds, still must Christ's wounds remain, for each new sin draws aside the curtain of another crucifixion. Christ is still on trial in the hearts of men, and every sin is another act by which Barabbas is preferred to Christ. There still are other Judases who blister His lips with a kiss, there still are other Pilates who condemn Him as an enemy of Caesar, there still are other Herods who robe Him in the garment of a fool, there still are gambling idlers who cast their dice, gambling away the riches of eternity for the baubles of time; there still are other Calvaries, for sin is the crucifixion over again. Arms that are outstretched to bless, we nail fast. Feet that would seek us in the devious ways of sin we dig with steel. Eyes that would look longingly after us as we set out for foreign countries, like other prodigals, we fill with dust. Lips that would speak to us words of tender pleading and forgiveness, we burn with gall. A heart that would pant for us as if we were fountains of living waters, we pierce with a lance. And when the last nail has been driven and Christ, like a wounded eagle, is unfurled upon His banner of salvation, we begin to say in our own heart of hearts that after all He could not be God, for if He were God how could we have crucified Him?

With the job of sinning done, which means the crucifixion, we make our way down the hill of Calvary and then there comes not the quake of earth but the quake of conscience which makes us say in our soul with the centurion, "Indeed, this is the Son of God." As uneasiness and remorse creep upon us, we look back to Calvary and wonder why He does not come after us. Why, if He is the Good Shepherd, does He not pursue His sheep? Why, if He is the Lord of all good gifts, does He not raise His hands to bless? Why, if He is the Lord of sinners, does He not bid us return to the foot of the cross?

Oh, tell me, how can hands bless that are nailed fast? How can lips that are bruised and parched with desolation preach the tidings of divine love? How can feet that are dug with steel go after souls that are lost? They cannot. And if we are to undo the harm that we have done, we must make our way up the penitential slope of Calvary, up to the chalice of all common miseries, and cast ourselves at the foot of the cross. We must kneel there at the foot of the pulpit of love and confess that when we stabbed His heart, it was our own we slew. But, oh, it is such a difficult thing to climb up the hill of Calvary! It is such a humiliating thing to be seen at the foot of the cross! It is such a painful thing to be with one in pain and to be seen with one condemned by the world! It is such a hard thing to kneel at the foot of the cross, and admit that one is wrong. *It is hard; but it is harder still to hang there!*

DYING AND BEHOLD WE LIVE

Dying and Behold We Live

Having delivered His farewell address from the pulpit of the cross and finished the work of His eternal Father, Jesus bows His head and dies. To make certain of His death, a centurion, Longinus by name, pierces His heart with a lance and the Divine Master, who saved up a few drops of His precious blood, now pours them out to prove that His love is stronger than death.

Two men who lacked courage to declare their affiliations while He was living, Joseph of Arimathea and Nicodemus, brought perfumes and spices and embalmed the body of Jesus. It was first laid on Mary's lap, and it seemed to her that Bethlehem had come back again — but really it had not. Between Bethlehem and Calvary our sins had intervened. The body was lifeless. Jesus was dead.

His enemies remembered that He had said that He would rise again, but they were certain He would not. They were afraid that the apostles would come and steal away the body and then say He had risen. Guarding against such deceit, they went to Pilate, asking him to set a watch of soldiers about the tomb for three days, in addition to which they would attach their own official seal to the stone before the entrance. Pilate acceded to their request. Then the evangelist Matthew fittingly closed his account of the Passion with the most ironic sentence in literature: "So they went and secured the tomb by fixing a seal to the stone and setting the guard." The seal was placed on the sepulchre, and a great stone was rolled in front of the door. His enemies took every precaution against fraud, but could take none against divinity. As they made their way down Calvary's hill, such thoughts as these ran through their minds: "Now, his fishermen can go back to their nets and their boats; their kingdom is a mockery. As for their master, his heart was so pierced that blood and water came from it. Even though he had a breath of life in that bloodless body, it is now being suffocated by the hundred-weight of spices with which he was embalmed. Our vigilance and that of the soldiers will not permit anyone to steal away the body. He who said he had life in abundance is now dead; he who said he could summon twelve legions of angels to his assistance now is cold as death; he who said he could raise up a child of Abraham from a stone is now buried under a stone. The impostor is dead! How wonderfully effective is a Roman death! Nothing can survive a crucifixion! He will never rise again!"

Is that true? Can one rise from the dead? Does

not the very fact that He was born in a stranger's cave and buried in a stranger's grave prove that human birth and death are equally foreign to Him? Look about at nature. Is not the springtime the Easter day of the Good Friday of winter? Has not all death within itself the germ of life? Does not the "falling rain bud the greenery"? Does not the falling acorn bud the tree? Why should all creation rise from the dead and not the Redeemer of creation?

"If this bright lily
Can live once more,
And its white promise
Be as before,
Why can not the great stone
Be moved from His door?
If the green grass
Ascend the shake
Year after year
And blossoms break
Again and again
For April's sake,
Why can not He,
From the dark and mold,
Show us again
His manifold
And gleaming glory,
A stream of gold?
Faint heart, be sure
These things must be.
See the new bud

On the old tree! …
If flowers can wake,
Oh, why not He?"

Sunday morning came, and it was one of calm, like the sleep of innocents. The clear, benign air seemed almost as if it had been stirred by angels' wings. Mary walked in the garden and someone near her spoke a word, and pronounced it longingly, wistfully, in that touching and unforgettable voice which had called her so many times: "Mary." And to this one and only word, she made an answer, a word and only one: "Rabboni." And as she fell at His knees in the dewy grass and clasped in her hands those bare feet, she saw two scars — two red-lined marks of nails, for Christ was now walking in the glory of His new Easter morn.

That was the first Easter day. Centuries have whirled away since, and on this new Easter day as I turn from that garden to the altar, I behold placed over the tabernacle, on this Resurrection day, the image, not of a Risen Savior, but the image of a dying one, to teach me that Christ lives over again in His Church, and that the Church, like Christ, not only lives, not only dies, but always rises from the dead. She is in love with death as a condition of birth, and with her, as with Christ, unless there is a Good Friday in her life, there will never be an Easter Sunday; unless there is the crown of thorns, there will never be the halo of light; and unless there is the cross, there will never be the empty tomb. In other words, every now and then the Church must be crucified by an unbelieving world and buried as dead, only to rise again. She never does anything but die, and for that peculiar reason she never does anything but live. Every now and then the very life seems to have gone out of her; she is pallid with death; her blood seems to have been sapped out of her; her enemies seal the tomb, roll a stone in front of her grave and say: "The Church will never rise again!" But somehow or other she proves them wrong; she does rise again.

At least a dozen times in history, the world has buried the Church and each time she has come to life again. We choose but a few such instances.

A hunted Savior must always have hunted children; and in those days of the Roman persecution the Church, like a mole, had to dig into the caves of the earth. There, under the foundation of Rome's proudest temples, under roads that rocked with the tramp of Rome's resistless legions, these children of God were nourishing themselves on the Bread of Life, fortifying their bodies as well as their souls, for the day when they would be led to the "thumbs-down" crowd of the Roman Colosseum to testify to their faith, even with their blood. The day came; they were led into the center of that great amphitheater with enemies round about; there was no escape, except from above — but that was enough. They met death with a smile upon their lips. Caesar's minions scattered fresh sands to hide their blood, but could not still their voice. It rose from the din of that arena; it entered into the very chancery of God's justice; it pierced the midst of undawned ages with no uncertain challenge: "In our blood has been mingled the blood of the living God, dying and behold we live." Roman swords blunted by massacre no longer fitted their sheaths; the wild beasts over-fed on the living flesh of the Church lost their craving for food, but still the bloody warfare went on. Caesar was certain he had conquered. He rejoiced that the Church was dead. Her life was sapped and drained; she could never survive the Roman sword. A stone was rolled before the door. The Church would never rise again. And as they set their watch, and even as they watched, the Church like her Risen Savior came from the grave of the catacombs and was seen walking in the glory of her new Easter morn.

There came other moments in her history when in the eyes of the world she seemed to have her very life drained of her. Whenever the Palm Sundays of earthly rejoicing came her way, and the world proclaimed her king, and strewed palm branches beneath her feet — in a word, whenever a great measure of temporal prosperity came her way, and she began to rely more upon action than prayer, she became weak. The yoke of Christ then seemed heavy to her children; bodies craved for the line of least resistance, and hearts yearned for the fleshpots of Egypt. It is a strange but certain fact that the Church is never so weak as when she is powerful with the world, never so poor as when she is rich with the riches of the world; never so foolish as when she is wise with the fancies of the world. She is strongest with divine help when she is weakest with human power, for like Peter she is given the miraculous draught of fishes when she admits by her own power she has labored all the night and taken nothing.

When her discipline, her spirit of saintliness, her zeal for Christ, her vigils, and her mortifications become a thing of less importance, the world makes the fatal mistake of believing that her soul is dead and her faith is departed. Not so! The faith, even in those days of lesser prayer, is solid, for it is the faith of the centuries: the faith of Jesus Christ. What may be weak is her *discipline*, her prayerfulness, and her saintliness, for these are of men, whereas her *faith* is of God. A renewal of spirit, then, will come not by changing her way of *thinking*, for that is divine, but her way of *acting*, for that is human.

But the world, failing to make this distinction between the divine and the human in her, as it failed to make it in Christ, takes her for dead. To the world, her very life seems spent; her heart pierced, her body drained; in its eyes she is just as dead as the Master when taken down from the cross, and there is nothing left to do but to lay her in the sepulchre. Once more a great stone is rolled before her tomb; the official seal of death placed upon it, the watch set; but as they watch, saintliness comes back, Christ stirs in Peter's bark, and at the very moment men are saying she is dead, she is seen walking in the glory of her new Easter morn.

With our own times came another death. Her death this time was inflicted not by executioners, but by other Pilates. These were dangerous days, for any civilization is in a bad way when it becomes indifferent, like another Pilate, to the answer to the question: "What is truth?" From inside and outside of the Church sprang up that old Greek error that there is no truth — an error, which for want of a knowledge of its ancient ancestry, was called Modernism. Truth was de-rationalized, error rationalized, and proofs brought forward to prove all proofs were worthless. Teachers who bedecked themselves in the robes of prophets became insulted if told they were not gentlemen, but remonstrated mildly if told they were not Christians. Minds now were told, and they began to believe, with the force of repetition, that we must be indifferent to both error and truth; that it is a lack of broadmindedness to make up one's mind; that it makes no difference whether God exists, whether Christ is God, or whether the sacraments do actually communicate divine life; the only thing that matters is the subjective impression such beliefs have upon the feeling of the believer. Minds began to live by catchwords, phrases covered up loose thinking, and there was hardly an ear that did not hear such catchwords and phrases as "Life is bigger than logic," and "The Christ of faith is not the Jesus of history."

The new spirit of the age was seemingly burying the Spirit of Christ. Books and articles were shot from the press, and in 1907 there hardly was an article written that did not say that the Church had now definitely reached its end. The world was asked to chant her requiem; a great stone was rolled before the door of her sepulchre; the watch set. "She would never rise again." And according to every human law she never should have risen from the dead! But for some mysterious reason the giant stirred. War was on. Long-range guns were tearing great, gaping wounds in majestic cathedrals; plowshares were beaten into swords; cannon fire changed poppy fields into Aceldamas of blood. And lo! And behold! That which was thought dead was seen on the battlefields pressing a crucifix to dying lips; and when the smoke of battle cleared and the mist lifted, she was seen walking in the glory of her new Easter morn; and even now as men watch her she grows! Christ, then, must have meant what He said when He declared that His Church would endure even to the consummation of the world.

There emerges, then, from her history one great and wonderful lesson, and it is this: Christ rose from the dead, not because He is man, but because He is God. The Church rises from the sepulchre in which violent hands or passing errors would inter her, not because she is human, but because she is divine. Nothing can rise from the dead except divinity. The world should profit by experience and give up expecting the Church to die. If a bell had been tolled on a thousand different occasions and the funeral never took place, men would soon begin to regard the funeral as a joke. So it is with the Church. The notice of her execution has been posted, but the execution has never taken place. Science killed her, and still she was there; history interred her, but still she was alive; modernism slew her, but still she lived.

Even civilizations are born, rise to greatness, then decline, suffer and die, but they never rise again. But the Church does rise again; in fact she is constantly finding her way out of the grave because she has a Captain who found His way out of the grave. The world may expect her to become tired, to be weak when she becomes powerful, to become poor when she is rich, but the world need never expect her to die. The world should give up looking for the extinction of that which so many times has been vainly extinguished.

Like a mighty oak tree which has stood for

twenty centuries, she bears fresh green foliage for each new age, that the age may come and enjoy the refreshing benediction of its shade. The flowers that open their chalices of perfume this spring are not old things, but new things on an old root. Such is the Church. She is reborn to each new age, and hence is the only new thing in the world. It is the errors that are old, for our so-called new thought is only an old mistake with a new label; it is not a new enthusiasm nor is it a new loyalty. The Church has put to bed all the errors of the past, for she knows that to marry the passing fads of any age is to be a widow in the next. She is therefore not behind the times, but beyond the times, always fresh while the age is dying.

She will go on dying and living again, and in each recurring cycle of a Good Friday and an Easter Sunday her one aim in life will be to preach Christ and Him crucified. As a student I may be expected to know something of her aims, and as her priest I may be expected to know something of her secrets, and I honestly assure you, at the close of this series, that the Church seeks not the overthrow of governments, desires not to impede progress, strives not to persecute those who differ with her (I know all these things are said about her). But what she does seek, with the full ardor of her soul, is to bring minds captive to the understanding of Christ, to lead wills to the glorious liberty of the sons of God, to thrill human hearts with the love that leaves all others cold, and to open eyes to a beauty that leaves all other beauty plain. And, hence, if any single word of mine has lifted up but one soul to a nobler understanding of Christ, or fanned a single spark of love for His cause into a flame, or induced the tendrils of a single heart to entwine about the Heart of hearts, then I shall believe that my words and my life shall not have been spoken or lived in vain.

The Church will go on, but its end and purpose will ever remain the same: to bring the peace of Christ to the souls of our countrymen. There will be no weapons to make that peace an armed peace, but there will be two insignificant instruments used, which have been used from the beginning, and they will be the instruments our Lord taught His apostles to use, namely those of fishermen and shepherds. I might say, therefore, we will go on "by hook and by crook," and the hook will be the hook of the fisherman, and the crook will be the crook of the shepherd; and with the hook we will catch souls for Christ, and with the crook we will keep them, even to the end of time; for as fishers of men and shepherds of souls we are committed to the high destiny of making Christ the King of human hearts, and with only the sign of Jonah the prophet, the fulfillment of that destiny can never be doubted, for *if Truth wins, we win; if Truth… Ah! but Truth can't lose.*